Table of Contents

Don't Put Up With Anxiety. Cure it!

Avigail Abarbanel

Fully Human Psychotherapy
http://fullyhuman.co.uk

Fully Human Psychotherapy Tools for Life Series
2017-2018

Don't Put Up With Anxiety. Cure it!

Booklet 2 in the 'Fully Human Psychotherapy Common Sense Tools for Life Series'.

Already published in this series: *Grief and Adjustment to Change, A no-nonsense approach*

Author can be contacted via http://fullyhuman.co.uk

Introduction

The kind of problems that bring people to therapy, depression, anxiety, lack of confidence, feeling lost or aimless, relationship problems, and so on, don't have to be permanent. For the majority of people such problems can be a thing of the past.

This booklet focuses on anxiety, which is not only common, but also seems to be on the rise. We hear just now that ever more children and teenagers are exhibiting signs of high anxiety. This is especially worrying because if nothing changes, these children might well grow into adults who will continue to experience anxiety.

Is this new, or is it just that we notice anxiety a lot more these days? We are certainly much more aware of emotional and mental health issues now than in previous generations. We also have names for things that were not named in the past.

I suspect that people have always suffered from anxiety. But maybe in the past people didn't know to complain about it. Maybe they thought this was just how life was for everyone, and this is the best they could hope for. Maybe they didn't think life could be any different. But we live longer now, and people rightly expect more out of life than our ancestors did. Being anxious and miserable so much of the time is not a good recipe for a fulfilling and productive life, especially if it's going to be a long one.

It's a good thing that we are not prepared to put up with things so much anymore, and that we are looking into what's going on with us with more focus, and in more detail. But when it comes to anxiety I am concerned that what people are told is largely unhelpful, and that most of what is on offer to help with anxiety is focused on symptom management.

Most people who go to their GP with anxiety are usually told that it's just something they have to live with, and that they'll have to learn to manage their anxiety. Many are offered potentially dangerous medication to control their anxiety. They are often not even told that the medication they're prescribed won't cure their anxiety, but that (if it works at all) it can only help with the symptoms. No one knows yet the long-term effects of the kind of drugs people are prescribed for anxiety and even in the short term, medication can have serious side effects.

As a psychotherapist one of the main things that bothers me about medication is that as long as people use it, they are not doing anything to deal with their real problems. They are just managing symptoms. This is unfortunate and unfair, because the majority of people are capable of much more than symptom management.

From clinical experience, I know that most people can live a fuller and more satisfying life without suffering from crippling anxiety. I believe that the symptom management approach to anxiety shows a lack of understanding of what is behind anxiety, and maybe also a lack of interest in helping people look deeper than the surface.

Most people are sane, which means that their emotional reactions are consistent with something. Emotions don't come out of nowhere and they are not a 'disorder'. Emotions always have a reason. If someone suffers from chronic anxiety, it is likely that there is a very good reason for it. It might not be obvious, but the reason is there nonetheless.

If you put your hand in a fire and it hurts, should you numb the pain with pain killers while letting your hand burn, or should you take your hand out of the fire? The pain and hurt we would feel if we did put our hand in a flame, is a natural response to a dangerous situation. The pain tells us something to which we must pay attention, or we could lose our hand… Emotions in general, and the experience of anxiety are also telling people something important. But instead of listening, people try to medicate the discomfort while doing nothing about the real cause of what they are feeling.

I didn't learn about anxiety from textbooks only. As a victim of childhood abuse who suffered from trauma, I grew up with chronic anxiety, in a chronically anxious environment. Looking back, I realise that I have not met many adults in my childhood who were not anxious. Anxiety was normal where I grew up. In addition to the abuse I suffered in my family, I was a member of a highly anxious society. Where there is a lot of trauma in a society for whatever reason, there is also a lot of anxiety. Children who grow up in an anxious environment will naturally feel anxious and insecure.

I know what it feels like to suffer from chronic Irritable Bowel Syndrome (IBS) for as long as I can remember. For years I thought everyone felt pain when they went to the toilet… I know what it's like to feel lost, panicked, and 'foggy in the head'. I know what it's like to feel shame about being anxious, and how much effort it takes to try to hide it. I know how humiliating, frightening, and exhausting it can be to live like this. I know the horrible despair that comes from believing that I might have to live like this for the rest of my life. I know intimately the up-and-down cycles that are a part of living with chronic anxiety.

I can't tell you the number of times I went to hospital truly believing there was something wrong with me, and that I was going to die from something horrible, only to be told (to my confusion and embarrassment) that there was nothing physically wrong with me. The thought that it was 'all in my head' was often worse than thinking I might have cancer or a brain tumour. If the doctors could identify something physical, then at least I could feel that there was a *reason* for how I was feeling. What a dreadful choice that was. Living with chronic anxiety, not understanding why it's there and thinking I was going crazy, or actually having some horrible illness…

I have deep empathy for anyone who suffers from chronic anxiety. I was there and came out the other end. I can tell you that there is life beyond anxiety, and that it is much freer, lighter, more peaceful, energetic and fulfilling.

Many people who live with chronic anxiety carry trauma from their childhood (as I did), that no one knows about, and that might have gone unnoticed over a lifetime. But trauma is not the only reason for anxiety. Even if your anxiety is not caused by childhood trauma, this booklet is still for you.

As you will read in this booklet, what we call anxiety is a result of the unskilled and, frankly, ignorant way that we handle our emotions. Of course, when children are abused, their emotions are abused. But most children's emotions are handled quite badly even where there is absolutely no abuse at all. In the majority of cases, once people learn what their emotions are and how to attend to them correctly, their anxiety first begins to diminish and then goes away completely. Anxiety is not the enemy. It is a useful wake up call or a nudge telling us to pay attention to something we have been neglecting in ourselves.

What I offer in this booklet is the same as what I offer to my clients. Everything in this brief booklet is based on years of experience both personal and professional, and on clinical evidence from many years of practice.

(If you do suffer from childhood trauma it's important that you seek the help of a psychotherapist who is experienced with trauma work. Please consider a professional who is interested in helping people heal properly, rather than someone who will teach you how to manage your symptoms.)

I hope you will find this booklet useful and helpful, and I wish you a full, fulfilling, and anxiety-free life.

I welcome feedback on everything I write. You can contact me through my practice website at http://fullyhuman.co.uk, or if you are a Facebook user, on my practice Facebook page. Just search Facebook for Fully Human Psychotherapy.

Avigail Abarbanel
Scottish Highlands
December 2017

Some Thoughts About Anxiety

As someone who has grown up with chronic anxiety, who recovered from it completely, and who regularly works with clients who suffer from anxiety, I am not that comfortable with the word 'anxiety'... I would prefer it if we called the experience of anxiety by its true name, *fear*. The truth is that people who feel anxiety are afraid. If they experience anxiety a lot it means they are afraid a lot.

Anxiety is a word that takes the legitimate emotion of fear and turns it into a pathology, a problem, something that is 'sick' or 'wrong' and that has no good reason to be there. Having said that, for the purpose of this booklet I will use the word 'anxiety', because that's what everyone calls it.

If someone is afraid of something, shouldn't we look at what they are afraid of, and try to help them with that, rather than try to make their fear go away? It might seem silly to you to say it this way, but sadly this is the approach that most people with anxiety encounter. Instead of seeing what's really going on for people that causes them to feel anxious (frightened), the anxiety itself is labelled the 'enemy' to get rid of.

I think we label fear 'anxiety' because anxiety can feel non-specific, or like it doesn't have a reason. When people know they are afraid they are often clear about what they are afraid of. But if everything seems OK, why would the person feel fear? Why would a person feel afraid when nothing obvious is going on or it looks like there is nothing to be afraid of? This non-specific fear became labelled 'anxiety', something abnormal, a 'condition', because it often cannot be linked to anything in particular, or at least, to anything obvious.

It's especially important to attend to your anxiety if you have children, or if you come in contact with children and young people elsewhere in your life. Children who are exposed to chronically anxious parents or significant adults can develop symptoms of trauma even if nothing is ever done to them, they are not abused, mistreated, or neglected in any way. When there is too much anxiety in a child's environment the child cannot relax and feel secure for long enough. Long term and recurring experience of insecurity in childhood is at the heart of what we call trauma.

Anxiety is Physiological

Anxiety is what we experience when the survival system in our brain is activated. When we face a threat, our entire system is conditioned by evolution to go into a state of emergency. This will affect how we feel in our body as it gets ready to fight, flee or play dead (freeze). We can experience palpitations as the heart starts to pump blood faster to move oxygen to vital organs and to our muscles. Our breathing will become shallower and faster. We might feel a need to run to the toilet as the digestive system begins to shut down, and the large intestine and the bladder would want to expel waste immediately. We can feel cold, shivery or tingly, temporarily lose our peripheral vision and develop tunnel vision. This helps to focus on the threat or on the escape route. We might feel dizzy, light-headed, experience blurred vision, a dry mouth, a sense of dread, fear and emergency, worry about things more acutely even if in reality they might not be that important, worry about how we are feeling and so on.

Our survival mechanisms and our fight-flight-freeze responses have evolved to ensure that we survive the next threat and live another day. The fight-flight-freeze responses are supposed to be short-term. They are a function of our mammal (limbic) brain and are there to save us from an immediate threat.

If each individual in a species has a strong drive to survive, the species as a whole would survive better. Our mammal brain is fear-based, and threat-focused. It doesn't 'care' if we are happy or fulfilled, good or bad, kind or ethical. Its only 'agenda' is the survival of our species.

We are here now and we are the way we are because of what worked for our ancestors. Those who survived passed on their genetic blueprint to us. Those who didn't survive long enough to have children, didn't get much of a chance to pass on their particular genetic makeup. Our species has so far been very successful at survival. Our numbers have been growing exponentially, and for better or worse, we have become the dominant species on our planet.

Our ancestors evolved on a hostile planet filled with predators and plenty of other threats and dangers from the physical environment, the climate and the elements, other members of their own species and other humanoids that existed at the same time. We became the dominant species on this planet partly because this survival system has worked for us. It worked because it was an adequate enough adaptation to our ancestors' harsh environment and it has enabled enough of them to survive and multiply.

Readers who have experienced or are experiencing anxiety regularly know what it's like. It can interfere with sleep, appetite, relationships, and with our thinking. In fact, when we are under threat our executive functions, such as rational thinking, planning ahead, decision-making, perspective, capacity for empathy, compassion, self-awareness, sense of purpose and direction and for being present for others, and so on, temporarily shut down. When our survival system is activated, we lose access to our higher, executive function in the prefrontal cortex of the brain because our mammal (limbic) brain temporarily shuts them down. We have evolved this way because it made more sense in the environment our ancestors lived in.

Without our executive functions, we were able to be more reactive, ruthless, aggressive, and therefore survive better. Without having access to a conscience, without feeling empathy for the predator or other humans that threatened us, without wasting time thinking, or seeking a purpose or a meaning for what was happening, without feeling concern for our impact on others, we were able to kill more easily, take what we wanted, or do whatever we had to do to survive another day. In that world, being ruthless and lacking empathy was a better guarantee of physical survival than concern for the welfare of those we had to harm or kill in order to survive. We all experience the way the limbic brain so easily takes over when we are under threat.

This might have helped us survive, but it doesn't mean it's comfortable or pleasant. When our executive functions are disabled we can also feel like a child, paralysed, lost, weak, frightened, agitated and reactive. We can feel unable to cope or function in situations which, given our age and abilities, we should be able to manage easily.

Because humans are not just wild unaware mammals, people tend to feel embarrassed and ashamed of their anxiety. They are afraid they are going crazy or 'losing it', or that they are 'weak', 'stupid', or can't 'cope'. Many people who experience chronic anxiety work hard to hide it from others because they are ashamed of it. Because anxiety blocks our executive functions, chronic anxiety can lead to an unfulfilling life. People describe it (and I remember it well) as *surviving* but not living.

Because of the temporary loss of executive functions when we experience a threat there is of course a real possibility that anxiety could interfere with important, responsible functions that people have to perform. If a pilot, a teacher, a nurse, or a surgeon are anxious, it would be hard or even impossible for them to think clearly and perform their tasks. Naturally this adds to people's worries.

It's exhausting to live with chronic anxiety, and it's likely to take a massive toll on the body and the immune system. When people experience anxiety, a cocktail of stress hormones (adrenaline and cortisol) that are responsible for our survival responses, flood the body. These chemicals are supposed to be used up if people fight, flee, or freeze. But if people do not fight, flee or play dead (because they are not really standing in front of a bear or a lion), and the anxiety is chronic, these hormones stay in the body unused and they can cause a variety of physical symptoms.

These physical symptoms might not be life threatening, but they can be uncomfortable or worrying. Irritable Bowel Syndrome (IBS), and fatigue are common symptoms in people who suffer from anxiety, but many other things can go wrong too. There is now growing evidence that our stress hormones could be responsible for much more serious illnesses. They are just not meant to flood the body all the time, only for short periods of time when we face a threat. The bodies of people who suffer from chronic anxiety are flooded with stress hormones all the time because their brain feels under threat all (or most) of the time.[1]

Anxiety Attack or Panic Attack?

A lot of people are not familiar with the professional terminology around anxiety, so I thought it's worth explaining it here briefly.

If anxiety levels are especially high, they can escalate into an *anxiety attack*. A *panic attack* is what happens when anxiety levels are very high *and* we also believe that there is something terribly wrong with us physically, to the point where we become convinced we are going to die. Clinically, a panic attack isn't just very high anxiety. It is what happens when we think we are actually going to die because we believe that the physical symptoms of anxiety are a real illness or medical crisis.

[1] To learn more about the physical impact of our stress hormones, I recommend the TED talk by Dr Nadine Burke Harris.

'Managing' Anxiety

You probably realise by now that I don't believe in managing symptoms. This section is therefore not about anxiety management techniques or strategies. It's about the common ways that people try to manage their own anxiety when they are still just coping with it.

Anxiety is so uncomfortable and can be so scary when you don't know much about it, that it is normal and natural to look for ways to manage it. This usually means trying to control or reduce it somehow. Everyone does it. It doesn't help if people go to professionals and get more of the same. It's not only uncomfortable and miserable to live with anxiety. Society can also make people feel that suffering from anxiety is a personal failure or a weakness of character and that it is 'wrong' or 'sick'. As a result, a lot more people than you might realise are hiding the fact that they are living with chronic anxiety.

There are a million ways that people try to reduce, manage, or 'medicate' anxiety. People use substances like alcohol, prescription and non-prescription drugs, smoking, or food, to try to control their anxiety. Almost any human behaviour or activity, even otherwise positive ones, can be used to try and manage or medicate anxiety. Activities like exercise, meditation, work, using computers and other gadgets, playing computer games, watching TV and movies, eating, socialising, cooking, sex, shopping, creative pursuits and hobbies, religion, can all be used to control or regulate anxiety. Eating disorders are also a way to try and manage anxiety, and so are self-harming and risk-taking behaviours, as well as obsessive compulsive and ritualistic behaviours. Generally, if a person is obsessed with something, it's useful to look behind the behaviour or preoccupation and check if there might be some anxiety there. I wonder if anyone has ever linked our obesity epidemic with the increasingly high levels of anxiety that people experience. I am not saying it's the only reason, but I have no doubt it plays a part.

Phobias are also a way for the mind to try and regulate or control high levels of anxiety — phobias are in fact clinically classified as 'anxiety disorders'. The human brain seeks consistency in everything and would always try to resist chaos and disintegration. Phobias and other preoccupations are the mind's way of channelling otherwise unexplained anxiety into something more tangible that can make sense, kind of...

People who experience anxiety often don't know what it's about. Sometimes they don't even know they are anxious. A phobia (and other, milder obsessive fears, compulsions or preoccupations) can in fact be a functional coping mechanism. The brain is simply trying to attach the anxiety to something that can make sense, like fear of flying, fear of spiders, or fear of crossing bridges or being in a crowd, fear of losing money or livelihood, to name but a few examples. All of these have an element of truth in them. Being killed by a spider, dying in a plane crash, losing one's livelihood, or being stuck on a bridge or in a crowd without being able to get away if something bad happens might be rare, but can in principle be real dangers. There is an element of truth in them, even if they are not common or likely in the person's day-to-day reality.

Activities used to medicate anxiety — as opposed to doing them just for pleasure or joy — would tend to have a quality of intensity and obsessiveness about them. This is different from just being passionate about an activity or a hobby.

Harmful activities or symptoms like phobias can obviously become a problem in themselves. This would only complicate things and can cause everyone to focus on the wrong thing. Instead of looking at what is driving these symptoms, the symptom itself becomes the focus of attention.

When you try to take these coping mechanisms away by trying to force people to stop using them, it would feel to them like you are trying to take away a crutch, the very thing that they feel helps them survive. It's why it can be so difficult for people to just stop a harmful behaviour, even when they know perfectly well that it's bad for their health, or that it's hurting others in their life. It's not because they are stupid or evil. (Most people are good and do the best they can with what they have and with what they know). It's because they don't know that they will survive without them. Their underlying anxiety is telling them that they are in danger. Without the crutch they fear they will not make it through another day.

The behaviour is there to *manage* and *control* something overwhelming and frightening, in this case anxiety. Until anxiety levels begin to diminish people would resist letting go of their crutch. If the crutch is taken away, or they decide to stop using it, they instinctively know they would have to face unbearable levels of anxiety. When people let go of a crutch without dealing with the anxiety that the crutch is managing, they can experience *symptoms substitution*. This means they will find another crutch and develop another symptom. The new crutch might be less harmful than the previous one, but the original problem is still there unchanged. A common example is substituting eating for smoking.

Many sufferers of eating disorders have told me over the years that they have resisted treatment or refused to follow an eating plan for example. They completely understand how a healthy diet can help them to be healthier. But they are afraid that once the symptoms of the eating disorder disappear, everyone would think they are now cured and that everything is OK. They know they are not OK and do not want people to think they are fine now just because they have lost all that extra weight, stopped binging and vomiting, or if they had anorexia, are eating properly and gaining healthy weight.

We know that all of these compensatory behaviours or crutches are effective. If they weren't, people wouldn't use them and they wouldn't be there. Studies on bulimia show that the cycle of binging and vomiting does make people feel better temporarily. Anyone who has experienced some self-medicating process or behaviour can vouch for that. The truth is that unless there is some payoff, some benefit to us, we wouldn't do it. We are primed for survival, not for self-harm and suicide, slow or otherwise. If people do something that is harmful or self-defeating, things must be really bad for them.

Medicating behaviours and consumption of substances can become full-blown addictions for some people. The brain always compensates for what we do or consume and does its best to adjust to whatever we put into it. Addictions develop when people need more of the same substance, behaviour or activity in order to get the same effect, and/or when people feel like they can't live without the substance, activity or behaviour they are addicted to.

If you look closely at people who have addictions you'll often find that there is more going on in addition to the obvious addiction. Although anxiety will be controlled and regulated to some degree by the person's addiction or other compensatory behaviour, it will still manifest in many other areas in the person's life. Our mind cannot be compartmentalised. We are a system and everything in us is linked to everything else.

The main problem with compensatory behaviours or crutches is that when people use them to medicate or control anxiety they don't deal with their anxiety at the core and don't see it for what it is. Since anxiety has a reason and a purpose, the more people try to mask or manage it, the worst it's likely to get. The addiction cycle is a successful and effective, albeit unsustainable, *deflection* from the real problem.

Some substances and some of the chemicals in food, like sugar, or salt for example, are also biochemically addictive. People can get into a vicious cycle that is hard and sometimes impossible to break. In some cases, as in drugs or alcohol abuse, people can cause permanent damage to the brain that cannot be repaired. It's tragic when people stop taking drugs or alcohol only to discover that their brain is now too damaged to rewire itself and change. Even with the best of intentions long years of consuming alcohol and drugs can lead to an inability to change (that is to heal and grow) because the brain just can't do it anymore.

Anxiety and Relationships

Anxiety is problematic for relationships. When we are anxious, the very qualities we need for healthy and connected relationships with others are temporarily impaired. As I explained above, when we are anxious – that is when we are triggered into survival – we have less access to our executive prefrontal functions. We have less access to compassion and empathy, to caring for others unconditionally, and to being able to reverse roles with others and see what it's like for them. We can't see clearly how we impact on others, and temporarily we might not even care about it. Anxiety makes us unavailable to others (and to ourselves), and we are likely to collapse into self-centredness and survival. When we are anxious we are just not 'all there'. For healthy, nurturing, and safe relationships we really need to be all there as much of the time as possible.

When things go wrong in relationships it is useful to reflect on how each partner manages their anxiety, or how anxiety is generally managed in the relationship. I know couples that sit and binge eat in front of the TV, or couples who binge drink together. This is likely to be their way of managing and regulating anxiety. It doesn't help that our commercially obsessed society makes it normal to binge eat or drink, because it drives people further away from looking at their anxiety.

Anything that people use to medicate or manage anxiety is likely to cause problems in relationships. Once people have an addiction, their main relationship is *with the addiction*. They are not emotionally available to be in a proper relationship with others. Managing what otherwise might be crippling anxiety feels to them much more urgent and more important than relating. When people are chronically anxious, relating can feel like a luxury they cannot afford because they feel like they are just surviving from moment to moment.

In AA (Alcoholics Anonymous) and similar programmes there is an emphasis on relationships as a key component in recovery. If people are able to put relationships with real people ahead of their fears, anxieties, compensatory behaviours and addictions, they are more likely to recover. Or better still, if people can be helped to deal with their anxieties within loving and safe relationships, they are more likely to succeed in recovering from addictions and healing the causes of their anxiety, whatever they might be.

What Really Causes Anxiety?

There is no simpler way to put this. Anxiety is what happens when feelings are not attended to or 'listened' to properly. It's therefore impossible to understand anxiety without understanding emotions and their dynamics. It is also why the key to living without anxiety is in learning how to attend to our emotions correctly.

Anxiety is a call for attention, a cry for help if you like, from our mammal (limbic) brain, that it needs the right kind of attention from our 'executive' adult brain, in the prefrontal cortex at the front of our brain.

Let's talk about feelings / emotions[2]

> "And you would accept the seasons of your heart, even as you have always accepted the seasons that pass over your fields. And you would watch with serenity through the winters of your grief."— **Khalil Gibran. *The Prophet*.**

If people could just do what Khalil Gibran suggests, no one, or hardly anyone would be anxious at all. But the reality is that most people have

---

[2] I use the world 'feeling' and 'emotion' to express the same thing.

no idea about the 'seasons of their heart', their emotions, what they are and how to handle them.

People bring different concerns to therapy. Whatever these concerns are, therapy is always about some kind of suffering, and suffering is always about emotions. Psychotherapy is almost always about people's relationship with their emotions. There is a recurring question that is almost always there whether clients ask it openly or whether it is hiding in the background: "Is this normal?" "Is what I am feeling normal?" All the clients I have ever met and I suspect a lot of people who don't go to therapy, *worry* about what they are feeling. The more uncomfortable the feelings are, the more people worry about them. (People don't tend to worry when they feel happy and satisfied.)

It's no wonder people worry about their feelings when our society is so unskilled and so poorly informed about them. In a misguided attempt to help, I think the medical and psychiatric professions have made things even worse. People are told that their uncomfortable feelings are 'mental health problems' and even a 'mental illness'. This makes emotional experiences like anxiety or depression sound abnormal, out of the ordinary, and terrifying.

I am not saying that there aren't people who have serious mental health problems. I just don't think they are as many as it would seem. They certainly are not the majority. Considering how widely anti-depressants and anti-anxiety drugs are prescribed, you'd think most people suffer from a mental illness. But this isn't the case.

In his group therapy theory Dr Irvin Yalom discusses the principle of 'universality'. Universality is the experience of not being alone with a particular problem we have. Most people tend to feel a little better just from knowing that someone else experiences something similar to them. This isn't *schadenfreude* — taking pleasure in someone else's misery. This is about the relief that comes from realising that others can understand what you are going through because they experience the same or something similar. It's about not feeling so alone in our suffering. Universality is what support groups are based on and the reason they are so helpful.

In one-on-one encounters therapists often use a micro-skill called 'normalising'. Normalising is the 'one-on-one' version of universality. It's letting clients know that what they experience is normal, that it is consistent with what happened to them and that there is nothing crazy, strange or sick about their feelings. Therapists spend a lot of time reassuring their clients that under the circumstances what they are feeling is completely normal.

But why do we worry so much about our emotions and whether they are normal or not? Even more importantly, why don't we all know already that what we feel is normal? We wouldn't spend nearly as much energy worrying about our feelings if in our childhood and youth we were regularly reassured that what we felt was normal. If during our childhood our caregivers were able to be *attuned* to our feelings accurately and make us feel 'felt' (as Dan Siegel wisely calls it); if the adults around us helped us develop an 'emotional vocabulary' – the language to name and express our feelings and inner experience – things would be very different for most of us later in life.

Children don't feel any less intensely because they are physically smaller. On the contrary. Up to about age fifteen most children operate almost exclusively from their mammal (limbic) brain. Their executive functions, which include emotional and behavioural regulation and self-awareness, are in development but they do not become reliable until much later. Children live in a fear-based, feeling world.

The limbic brain's 'agenda', 'mission' or 'purpose' is the survival of our species. It's not 'interested' in whether we are happy or not, or if our lives are fulfilling or satisfying. It 'cares' only that we survive long enough to procreate, protect our young so they live long enough to have more babies, so that our species can continue. The limbic brain is designed by evolution to worry about unpleasant and uncomfortable feelings because an uncomfortable feeling is associated with something bad or threatening that might be happening to us.

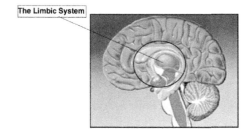

The Limbic System

Human children are vulnerable for a lot longer than the young of other species. They look to adults for protection and safety right into early adulthood. Children do not have enough life experience so they look to adults to teach them what's worth worrying about and what isn't. If they are taught incorrectly, they will carry the same childhood fears and anxieties with them into adulthood, often without the language to express them, or the ability to make sense of them. Children need to be taught what their feelings mean and be reassured that they are consistent with what is happening to them.

Feelings have had a reputation as unreliable, volatile, and the opposite of common sense and reason. For millennia and in some places even now, women were seen as more 'emotional'. This was an excuse to think of women as fickle, unreliable, child-like, and less intelligent than men, and to treat us as inferior. Males were traditionally assumed to be less emotional, more rational and therefore more reliable or intelligent. It's nonsense of course, but it tells you a lot about our attitude to emotions.

Emotions have been denied, ignored, ridiculed, abused, pushed away, and suppressed, not to mention medicated with drugs of all kinds throughout our existence. I find that in every family and in every society, there are emotions that are more acceptable and emotions that are not. We regularly discriminate between emotions that we consider 'acceptable', 'good', 'healthy' or 'OK', and those we consider 'bad', 'sick', 'dangerous', or 'unacceptable'.

Our difficult relationship with our uncomfortable emotions is, I believe, also a legacy of generations of misinformation, and incorrect understanding of emotions, what they are, and what they are for. Why are we so poorly informed and why don't we learn this at home as children? The simple answer is that parents and adults in general can't teach what they don't know. Until we know better, ignorance and bad practice continue to be passed down through the generations.

There is no such thing as 'negative emotions'

Every time I hear or read the phrase 'negative emotions' it makes me cringe. It shows such a lack of understanding of what feelings are. No matter how uncomfortable or bad they feel, emotions are not a problem to be solved, or something to change or eliminate.

Emotions are *information*, and they are always there for a reason. The reason can be outside or inside of us, or both. Either way there is always a reason. Emotions provide a substantial proportion of the information that we need in order to be well, make good decisions, survive, and thrive. To ignore feelings is irrational. Feelings are the limbic brain's ancient 'language', the way it tries to do its job, which is to communicate information that could be vital to our survival. All mammals feel but as far as we know we are the only species of mammal on the planet that *worries* about how we feel.

Think of the limbic brain as similar to the radar that you see in every airport, the one that turns and turns and never stops. The radar's role is to scan the airspace around the airport and alert us to anything that might be up there, a flock of birds, a storm, or aircraft. The radar uses radio waves to scan the airspace. As the radio waves move out, they bounce off anything solid in the airspace that could be a threat to aircraft. When the radio waves bounce back from something, this translates into dots on the radar screen in the air traffic control tower. The air traffic controller makes sense of these dots, and then makes skilled decisions that keep everyone safe. The air traffic controller *understands* what the dots on the screen mean and uses the information they provide to make good decisions for the purpose of safety.

Our limbic brain works in a similar way. It continuously scans our inside (our body) and our outside (our environment) using our five senses. When it encounters something, especially a potential threat, it will try to 'report back' with a feeling. Our feelings are like the dots on the radar screen. They are saying something that we need to know.

Our safety in the air depends on the correct interpretation of those dots on the radar screen, and on the decisions made by air traffic controllers. We trust that air traffic controllers pay attention to *all the information, all* the dots they see on their screens, and that they know the right action to take in different situations. We can't afford for air traffic controllers to randomly ignore dots they don't 'like', or don't 'feel like' attending to. Imagine if an air traffic controller looked at one of those dots on the radar, and thought, 'I really don't like this dot, so I'm just going to ignore it' or, 'I'm scared of this dot, so I'll turn away from it and pretend it isn't there'… This is what we are like with so many of our emotions. Is there any wonder we suffer from so many 'crashes' internally and things can feel so messy and unsafe?

Instead of realising what our emotions are, and how important they are, we tend to ignore or push away those we don't like, those we are afraid of, or aren't comfortable with, or those we believe would be unacceptable to others. How many disasters and how much chaos would be in our airspaces if air traffic controllers did the same thing?

Yet flying is still the safest mode of travel we have, and it's to a large part due to these very skilled individuals who do their work properly, and whom we trust with our lives. But our psychological 'air space' isn't that safe or peaceful. It's filled with 'accidents' and 'crashes'. Many people's psyches are not safe spaces with a safe flow of experience and information. Therapy is where a lot of people seek help when the inner world feels troubled and messy. When we hear that mental health issues are on the rise, it means that things are getting worse in our psychological airspace, and it's because we are not doing it right.

Are feelings primitive, or part of a primitive system? Probably, considering that our limbic brain is ancient. If we continue to evolve, would we lose our capacity to feel in another hundred million years? I don't know, and I hope we don't. Our feelings have a way of offering 'colour' and 'texture' to our life, and to what we experience. At the same time as we suffer or feel uncomfortable when we experience threat, our feelings also enable us to experience pleasure, wonder, enjoyment, attachment and joy.

It looks like society would like to get rid of our 'bad' feelings. A lot of people mistakenly think that therapy is about 'feeling better'. They come to therapy hoping that somehow I'd help them feel less of the uncomfortable stuff. One of my clients once asked me half-jokingly if I could 'amputate' that part of him that feels so awful. Trying to get rid of uncomfortable feelings is like trying to convince your body to never pee again.

There are no shortcuts to enlightenment, maturity or wellbeing. Because of how our brain is made, we cannot bypass or ignore feelings, no matter how uncomfortable they are. In fact, the more uncomfortable our feelings are, the more we should pay attention. But having uncomfortable feelings doesn't mean we are 'sick'.

The mammal (limbic) brain's job is to communicate information about our inside and outside environments, in order to keep us safe. But it can only interpret this information based on its past experiences.

Our mammal (limbic) brain is limited by what it has experienced or witnessed. It is not able to look beyond. It is a reactive brain that is careful and conservative and sticks to what it knows. The reason it's like this now is because it has worked for our ancestors.

The stronger the past experience was, the more fear or suffering it might have triggered at the time, the more strongly it would be wired into our limbic system. From a limbic point of view, we are always at the mercy of interpreting the present from the point of view of our past. We often feel about the present what we felt in our past, even if rationally we can see that our present is very different from the past we grew up in, or otherwise experienced. If a friend betrayed you and it was a devastating experience at the time, it would be natural to be cautious about new friendships because it could happen again. We learned well from experience and it was sensible for our ancestors, but we can also limit ourselves because of our past experiences. The important point is that if, or when this happens, we need to remember that our limbic brain is simply doing its job.

Each person carries unique sensitivities depending on their past, and the experiences that were wired into their brain. So, we don't all react the same way to the same situation. We react to what *our own particular* limbic system interprets as dangerous or a problem, based on *our own particular history*. We react not because we are bad, crazy, unreasonable, stubborn, or stupid. We react because this is what our limbic brain has evolved by nature to do in the environment that first shaped us.

The limbic system is entrusted with our physical survival. If the information it tries to communicate is not transmitted to where it's supposed to, if it is not received or acted on properly, if the limbic brain is left to deal with this information on its own, it will result in the limbic brain feeling unsure about our survival. It is likely then to spiral into even higher alert and panic.

The limbic brain might be trying to warn us of something but no one is listening and no one is doing anything about the information it communicates. Think of the last time you saw a child or a teenager escalate their behaviour. That's because young humans expect the brains of the adults around them to *receive the information* that their limbic brain is communicating, and do whatever is necessary to keep them safe.

The young of our species are entirely dependent on adults for their survival. But adults often do not have any idea what's happening inside children's inner world. Even if they do, many adults don't know how to handle the child's inner experience correctly, and the child can spiral into deeper and deeper fear and terror. Children feel *fear* when their uncomfortable emotions are not handled correctly. Their limbic brain has no confidence that they would survive. As we grow into adults who do not know how to handle feelings (because we were never shown how to) we experience that old fear from childhood as anxiety.

Feelings and behaviour

Perhaps we confuse emotions with our (limbic) *reaction* to them — what we are habitually or instinctively wired to *do* when we feel something. While the limbic system gives us our emotions, or in other words, information about what's going on, the *choice* about how to behave in response to these feelings should not be left for the limbic brain to make. In a world without sabre tooth tigers and ice ages, our choices and decisions should ideally come from our executive brain.

The limbic system has evolved for short-term, moment-to-moment survival. It doesn't have the ability to 'think' rationally, plan well for the future, or take a lot of information into account in its decision-making. It tends to be limited to a narrow range of options, most of which we developed in our early childhood. They are our own unique variations on the automatic and ancient fight-flight-freeze threat responses. So, when we see adults behave out of their limbic brain in response to an emotion they happen to feel, it often doesn't look great... We accept children making bad decisions and not seeing the 'bigger picture', but we expect adults to behave differently. Moreover, adult decisions can carry much more weight and significance and have a much bigger and far reaching impact than decisions made by children.

If we grow up with a parent who had a frightening tantrum each time they felt annoyed or disappointed, we can become wary of the emotions that led to that behaviour. What we learn is that *these kinds of emotions lead to this kind of behaviour.* We might conclude that anger leads to aggression and violence, impatience or frustration lead to tantrums, pain leads to becoming drunk, sadness or grief lead to collapse, and so on. It all depends on what we saw around us when we were growing up.

As I mentioned earlier, in most people emotions are *consistent* with real life events. The limbic brain is *reactive*, and emotions are a reaction to something. It could be past or present events, or both. Either way, in the vast majority of cases emotions *make sense* and are connected to something. Most people are sane, so most people's emotions make perfect sense if you know something about their past or present circumstances. Treating emotions separately from the context of a person's history or present reality is harmful because it can reinforce the belief that those emotions are 'sick' or 'wrong'. It can and does make people feel even more 'crazy' or 'strange' than they already do. This can be soul destroying.

About the dynamics of emotions / feelings

Any emotion we try to block in ourselves and in others will try to 'push' through anyway. From our limbic system's point of view, our lives might depend on the emotion being communicated properly. The feeling won't just go away, it will try to complete its cycle because in times of threat, survival is top priority. This is especially true for strong emotions. Strong feelings can be triggered because something in the present is perceived as a serious threat. They can also be caused by something from the past that was a threat back then, that is triggered or *resonates* with something in the present.

An important rule of thumb to remember is that if feelings are *overwhelming*, they are likely to be 90% in the past and only 10% in the present. Feelings that are just about the present and have no links to anything in the past, will not feel overwhelming or particularly intense. They will also fade away fairly quickly and will not be much of a problem.

A Rule of Thumb

If feelings are overwhelming, they are probably 90% in the past and only 10% in the present.

A trigger is what happens when (from a limbic point of view) there is *enough* similarity between something that is happening now and something threatening from the past. This is true even when objectively, there is nothing in the present that poses an actual threat to survival.

Even if it is only a trigger and nothing threatening is happening now, limbic brain must communicate its message. If the message doesn't get through, the limbic system will continue to think that we are at risk and will not stop until we pay attention.

Displaced anger is a good example of this. If your boss at work made you angry and you couldn't communicate it to her or sort it out with her, you might end up taking it out on your partner and children when you get home. You might pick on something they said or did. In that moment, you will truly believe that it is what they are saying or doing that's making you angry. If the emotion is overwhelming, you might need to consider that it's not even the boss that is the real source of your anger. Rather what happened with your boss triggered something even older from your more distant past.

Emotions are often out of awareness. People might realise they were angry only *after* they have already blown up in the wrong place or time or at the wrong people (not the blowing up is the right thing to do even with the right people). Losing our temper can hurt others and is likely to also feel confusing to us.

Other examples of unacknowledged or blocked emotions trying to push through to complete their natural cycle can be when sadness, grief or helplessness develop into depression, or when anger transforms into rage, muscle pain in the neck, upper arms, upper back or shoulders, or into a headache.

The diagram on the next page shows the dynamic of emotions. A trigger would cause an emotion to start. Anything can be a trigger. It all depends on people's unique history and what is wired into their limbic brain from their childhood and life experiences. The emotion would then escalate and reach a peak. If it's heard properly it would complete its natural cycle. If the emotion is allowed to complete its cycle it's quite common to get an insight about it. It's the moment when we understand *why* we feel the way we do.

If we block the emotion, the cycle cannot complete itself and the information is not transferred or received successfully. Most people come to therapy with a huge number of 'blocked' emotions that have not been allowed to complete their cycle. Blocks can be caused by messages that people give to themselves or others. The list below the graph offers a few examples. Can you identify anything familiar in that list? What would you add to it?

The circle at the bottom of the diagram is saying that because the human mind always seeks completion, emotions will not go away and will somehow try to complete their cycle.

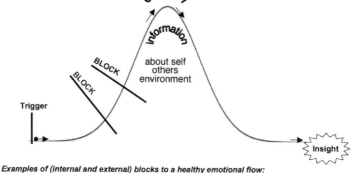

The Dynamics of Emotions

Examples of (internal and external) blocks to a healthy emotional flow:
- WHY do you / I feel like this?
- I don't have time for this. I have things to do.
- What's the point of feeling this?
- Boys don't cry!
- It's not nice for girls to be angry.
- I hate feeling angry / sad / hurt / disappointed
- You're upsetting your mother / father.
- I / you SHOULD be over this by now.
- I don't want to be seen as weak.
- What will people think of me?
- I SHOULD be happy.
- Others have bigger problems. I don't have a right to feel this.
- I'm scared that if I start crying I'll never stop.
- I MUST do / eat something to cheer myself up.
- I'm scared to feel like this.
- Feeling anything other than happy is wrong / sick, etc....

Assumption:

Emotional, behavioural or physical problems are symptoms of a lifetime of blocked emotional cycles.

Note: If the normal emotional cycle is not allowed to be completed, it will try to complete itself somehow!

the human mind seeks completion

Identify Your Blocks

• What feelings are you more likely to block in yourself or in others?

• Who taught you or how did you learn to block those emotions?

• How do you block them? What do you tell yourself or others, or what do you do to stop yours or someone else's emotions?

• What do you worry might happen if you didn't block those emotions and if you allowed them to complete their cycle?

The Childhood Origins of Anxiety

What do you imagine children experience when they feel something uncomfortable and the adults around them either do not notice, or mishandle (block) their feelings? A child whose feelings are not noticed, or whose feelings are mishandled in some way by significant adults, will feel abandoned and will therefore feel fear. Children are always afraid when they feel something uncomfortable. They operate mostly out of their limbic brain and the limbic brain associates uncomfortable feelings with a possible threat or danger. If adults ignore or mishandle children's feelings in any way, children feel abandoned to their fear and sense of threat and danger.

The fear of a child whose uncomfortable feelings aren't handled properly or go unnoticed will escalate, and the child is likely to express this in his or her behaviour. Some children act out what they feel to try to be noticed, while others can collapse internally. Either way children don't have a choice about it. If children act out there is *always* a reason and it's important that everyone around them pay attention. Children are not 'naughty' or 'annoying'. They try to communicate something, but they need help to do it effectively, which means that they need to know that they are heard and seen.

Children always try to communicate how they feel because they need to survive, and because their survival depends on the adults around them. They will do anything to try and get the message across. What people interpret as annoying behaviour, or some kind of acting out, is likely to be there because the child's feelings are not heard or not handled properly. This can be either in the moment, or because the child's repeated experience with their significant adults has already taught them that their feelings are never heard and are often mishandled.

Children are not in a position to say to adults, '*You need to validate how I feel, because this is what my limbic brain needs in order to feel that you have heard my problem and that you'll keep me safe*'. Children don't have that kind of awareness yet, so they will try to express what they need the best way they know how.

Anxiety in adulthood is a direct result of learning the wrong lessons in childhood about our emotions and how to handle them. Even people who grew up in non-abusive families can grow into adults with a limbic brain that is wired to mishandle emotions in any of the ways in the table below or others.

Mishandling children's (or anyone's) feelings can take the form of trying to **distract, interrogate** or **demand that they explain 'why'** they feel the way they do, **making fun** of the feelings, **mocking** or **shaming**, **dismissing** them, **belittling** or **minimising**, **comparing** the person's feelings to someone else's, **trying to control** or **criticising** the feeling, **accusing**, **using emotional pressure, threatening**, **rationalising** the feelings away, **ignoring**, **rejecting** the feelings or **brutalising** the person.

The table on the next page shows examples of how children's feelings can be mishandled. Most of these examples come from what clients have told me over the years about how their feelings were treated by significant adults in their childhood. Some come from my own experience, and some from what I witness when I see interactions between adults and children. (Feel free to add more categories and examples from your own experience and observations.)

Examples of incorrect approaches to emotions

Distracting	• "Come on, let's play with your new toy lorry" • "Let's have your favourite ice cream. That will make you feel better." • "Go do something useful. You'll feel better."
Interrogating	• "*Why* are you feeling like this?" • "You have to explain to me why you are feeling this way, because I can't see any reason for it."
Making fun of the feeling / mocking / shaming / humiliating	• "Oh, look at her, she is a sour puss again..." • "Ha, ha, here start the waterworks again..." • "Always with the drama" ... • "Oh, God, here we go again" ... • "What are you a girl? What a wuss?"
Dismissing	• "Don't be silly of course your friends like you" • "Do you have any idea what it was like for me when I was your age? I had something to be sad about but you have you have everything you need. You don't have any reason to be upset." • "Are you upset again? I really don't have time for your drama and moods!" • "Stop this and go do your homework." • "It's all in your head."
Demonstrating impatience / lack of interest	• "I don't have time for one of your moods now. You know how busy I am..."
Belittling, minimising	• "You are upset about this? Don't be silly, it's nothing." • "Silly billy" ... • "You always make such a big deal of things..."
Comparing	• "Your sister doesn't react like that?" "Why can't you be more like her?"
Controlling	• "What are you so happy about? We both know it will all end up in tears."

	• "In this family I am the only one who is allowed to get angry."
Criticising	• "Why can't you just be happy? Why do you have to be upset?" • "What's wrong with you?" • "Are you stupid or something?" • "You shouldn't feel like this." • "You need to be stronger than this. Be brave."
Accusing	• "Whatever it is, you must have done something to deserve it..."
Using emotional pressure	• "You know that I don't like to see you sad. It makes me upset." • "Look what you did. You made everyone upset now." • "Are you saying that I am not a good mother?" • "You are upsetting your father." • "You're ruining it for everyone."
Threatening	• "Don't you dare be angry with me, I am your mother/father". • "How dare you!" • "Just do as you are told, or else" ... • "I'll give you something to cry about!"
Rationalising	• "It doesn't make sense to feel upset about this. You need to think about this differently..." • "You're overreacting." • "What's the point of feeling like this? It won't get you anywhere. You need to concentrate on the positives."
Ignoring	The adult care giver is there but is indifferent, and does not engage with the child at all, walks out of the room, continues to do their activity, turns their face away from the child, or keeps their back turned, etc.
Rejecting	• "Go to your room until you feel better and come back when you can put a smile on your face." • "If you are going to cry, go cry in your room."

	• "I don't want to see you like this. Go wash your face and come back here."
Punishing (psychologically)	The adult gives the child the 'cold shoulder'. Punishes the child for feeling something the adult doesn't like by withdrawing. It is a way to force the child to change how he or she feels. This is also a form of rejection and control.
*Brutalising / using violence **(*Although this is illegal in the West, it is still done behind closed doors.)**	• "This (slap, smack or other brutal behaviour) will give you something to cry about." • "If you keep being like this I'm going to send you away." • Locking a child away in a room or worse.

In many cases children's feelings are treated as if they aren't feelings at all, but rather a problem *behaviour*. In other words, when children *feel* something that adults don't like or that makes adults feel uncomfortable, children are given the message that just by *feeling* something they are *doing* something wrong or are hurting someone. This teaches children that feelings and behaviour are the *same thing*, when of course they are not.

Children who grow up like this can turn into adults who believe that when they feel something, they are hurting other people. So, for example, if a feeling of anger was not allowed in the family, children can grow up to believe that feeling angry is wrong, regardless of how they act when they are angry.

Children rarely follow only what they are told. We have evolved to learn best by imitation, by watching what others *do*. Children can develop a negative impression of some feelings because they witness the adults around them mishandle their own emotions. So, if an angry parent behaves violently, children can grow up into adults who avoid their own anger. This is because they associate anger with violence. Many clients have told me over the years, 'I don't *do* anger, I'm not an angry person. When my father was angry he used to punch the walls and yell at us. I don't want to be like him'... Alternatively, of course, a child can grow up into an adult who also lashes out violently verbally or physically when angry. This is how anger was expressed in the family and this is what the child experienced as normal.

If a parent collapsed each time they felt sad or hurt, children can grow up believing that sadness or hurt are dangerous, because they cause people to collapse and not cope. They would either suppress these feelings as best they can, or alternatively collapse and not cope, because they never learned how to be OK with feeling sad or hurt.

Parents' inner worlds provide a blueprint for their children's inner worlds. This is because the wiring of the parents' brain provides a blueprint for the way their child's brain will be wired. Whether they like it or not, parents cannot take their children further than they themselves have come developmentally. Children tend to leave home with a similar level of development to their parents.

The way parents or significant adults handle their own feelings *internally* becomes the basis for children's attitude to their own emotions. For example, a parent who is kind with her child's feelings, but not her own, sends a confusing message that there is one rule for the child, and a different one for the parent. What children would learn is exactly that, that there is one rule for them and another rule for other people. When these children grow up they are likely to repeat what the parents did, that is be kind to others but not to themselves. I have seen too many examples of this over the years.

People suffer when they treat themselves badly internally and are not kind to their own feelings. Children sense all of it, even if they don't know the details. No child wants to see their caregivers or parents suffer. From the child's perspective, a suffering adult might not be able to be strong or fit enough to protect them. This can lead to children becoming 'parentified', that is spending their energy taking care of their parents' emotions to try to ease the parents' suffering. They do this in the hope that eventually their parents would be able to take care of them. Alternatively, parentified children can grow into adults who disrespect their parents or anyone in position of authority because they perceive other adults as weak and unreliable.

Ideally adults who care for children should have a reasonably peaceful inner world. This doesn't mean not having 'issues'. It means not having too much internal conflict, not having bits of themselves fighting internally with other bits of themselves. Adults who are in a state of war with themselves are bound to suffer from anxiety. High levels of anxiety in adults can lead, not only to anxiety but even to trauma symptoms in children[3]. Trauma is caused by a long-term inability to relax, and children do not feel secure around adults who are anxious, even if those adults are otherwise kind to others.

Because children's inner world ends up mirroring their parents' inner world, inner conflict in parents is likely to lead to inner conflict that children would carry with them into adulthood. Of course, inner conflict means anxiety...

My message here is not that people should not or cannot have problems or issues. No one is 'issue-free' and having issues does not automatically disqualifies people from being good parents. The message is rather that parents, (or anyone who looks after children), must have a firm and ongoing *commitment* to their own personal growth and development. Anything parents or adults in general *avoid* in themselves will affect children negatively.

Even without any abuse, when children's feelings are handled clumsily or carelessly, they are likely to feel that they are not loved or wanted. The truth is that their instinct is in fact correct. Parents who love their children but mishandle their feelings on a regular basis, are not *acting* lovingly. Children depend on love, and love isn't just a warm

---

[3] You can read more about trauma and what causes it in my booklet, *Trauma and Its Impact: What you need to know.*

and fuzzy feeling, caring for the physical needs of the child, or engaging with the child intellectually. *Love is expressed in the most powerful and long-lasting way in how we respond to the emotions that others express to us.*

Can you see how confusing it can be for children who are told regularly that they are loved, but whose feelings are also regularly mishandled? What are they supposed to make of it? They are told they are loved, but when they come to the parent with a difficult emotion they need help with, they do not *feel* loved because of the parent's clumsiness with the emotion.

Children would do anything to be accepted and approved of. If feeling sad isn't acceptable in the family, children would learn to push sadness away, and put a smile on their faces in order to be accepted. This would cause the particular emotional experience to go into a kind of 'quarantine' in the brain. It will remain as an unprocessed and unintegrated cluster of neurons in the limbic brain. Because these clusters of neurones are not integrated properly, they remain there as a potential 'time bomb' or 'landmine' that can explode whenever the right trigger is pressed. We are likely to experience it as out of our awareness or control because it *is* usually out of our awareness and control...

When so many emotional experiences are quarantined over many years of being mishandled in the same way, it's easy to see how people can grow into adults who are 'out of touch' with themselves. Most parents' own unintegrated limbic material can get triggered when their children feel something uncomfortable. Parents are more likely to react out of their own childhood wiring, often doing to their child what was done to them in their own childhood, even if it's the last thing they want to do. If the material is out of awareness (unintegrated) they simply would not be able to help it.

The kind of feelings that anxiety masks underneath can include anything that was not acceptable in the child's original environment. Some people can even feel anxious when they are happy or feel pleasure, because being relaxed or feeling pleasure was frowned upon in their family. I used to feel anxious even when I was happy or something good happened to me. When I was growing up I was told not to enjoy good things too much because something bad was going to happen to "balance things out". The adults around me often made sure that something bad did happen after something good happen to me. I learned that if something good happens, something bad always followed and therefore learned to fear feeling good, relaxed or happy.

It's not one particular feeling or another that's the problem. It is the experience of not being allowed to feel whatever was not allowed or accepted in our original environment. It is different for each one of us.

Anxiety is a blessing in disguise. It is the last option left to our limbic brain to communicate something important. If you feel anxiety think of it as a younger version of yourself trying to draw your attention. Something you are feeling is not being attended to properly.

Learning Good Emotional Skills

- Next time someone (a partner, colleague, friend, a child) tells you how they feel about something, notice what you say in response. What is your *habitual* response to other people's feelings?
- Do you feel an obligation to make the person 'feel better', or help them out of their emotion somehow?
- Do you consider an uncomfortable emotion a *problem* to be solved?
- Reflect on where you've learned to respond to other people's emotions the way you do. Was it done to you? Did/do you see others around you acting this way with each other?
- Next time someone tells you how they feel, try to validate their emotion. Validation means telling someone that it's OK to feel the way they do.
- Pay close attention to how it feels for you to do it. What do you notice about your own inner experience when you validate someone else's emotion? (Is it comfortable, uncomfortable, does it feel silly or pointless, is it easy or difficult, do you feel helpful or unhelpful?)
- What do you notice about the other person's reaction after you have validated their emotion?

Non-Emotional Causes of Anxiety

There are things that have nothing to do with emotions that can create anxiety-like symptoms. One of them is stimulants such as caffeine. Too much caffeine can lead to similar physical reactions to anxiety. Any external source of adrenaline such as the adrenaline that some local anaesthetics contain (the kind that is sometimes used by dentists) can cause anxiety-like symptoms. Since too much adrenaline can take its toll on the body, it's a good idea not to consume too much caffeine or other stimulants. As for the dentist, the effects of adrenaline from the local anaesthetics usually wears off pretty quickly.

Women can sometimes get anxiety-like symptoms during PMT (Premenstrual Tension). It is unpleasant but it passes as the hormonal cycle moves on. When adrenaline leaves the body it's common to feel physically tired and deflated.

Some degree of anxiety is normal. For example, before performance it's normal to experience some anxiety, which I tend to think of as excitement. (Fritz Perls, one of the fathers and developers of Gestalt therapy said that anxiety and excitement are two sides of the same coin.) Performance anxiety is useful because we need that extra adrenaline to ready us to do what we are about to do, sing, play an instrument, perform in a play, give a speech, teach, give an interview or chair a meeting. This kind of anxiety is usually not paralysing and debilitating. As soon as the activity starts, it dissipates and we become focused on our task.

How to Cure Anxiety?

The theory for curing anxiety is simple, but it takes a lot of practice and requires learning new emotional skills. In order for anxiety to be cured, the executive part of our brain needs to learn the correct way to respond to our feelings. These are the responses that should have been there in our childhood environment but weren't.

Remember that most parents do the best they can, but they can't teach what they don't know. Whatever we didn't learn growing up in our family, we would have to learn as adults. Thanks to 'neuroplasticity' our brains continue to wire and rewire themselves all through our life. This means that we can learn new emotional skills and practices at any stage in life.

As the executive part of our brain begins to 'listen' to the feelings that are coming from our limbic brain, as it begins to respond to them in the right way, anxiety will begin to diminish.

To change anything about ourselves in a permanent and lasting way means to change something in our brain. To change our brain's 'architecture' (how it is wired) requires attention, correct practice, and a lot of repetition. The practice I offer in the next page is hard work, not a quick fix.

The key to working correctly with emotions is **Validation.** Validation is telling ourselves that all of our feelings are OK, that it's OK to feel the way we do. This internal validation has to come from our executive brain. To live anxiety-free, all of our feelings must become OK for us to feel. I am talking about much more than 'tolerating' our feelings. I am talking about seeing our emotions as a valuable source of information and developing the skill to work with them the right way.

The practice

- It begins with noticing when you feel something. Sometimes you might feel it first in your body before you notice it in your emotions. If you find it difficult to notice your emotions, pay attention to your body-sensations first. If you can't name your emotions or your body-sensations don't worry about it. It will come with time.

- Take a deep breath or a few deep breaths. Don't work too hard at it. Just breathe a little more deeply than usual. The breath is important because it will enable you to get access to your executive brain where your executive functions are. It's this part of your brain that is supposed to learn to validate your emotions.

- As you feel yourself slightly more centred and grounded, tell yourself that what you are feeling is OK, that it is OK to feel the way you do. Speak as if you speak to someone else. It might feel strange at first, but it works. It doesn't matter if you can't name what you feel. The validation needs to be unconditional. *All your feelings*, whatever they are, are OK.

- If you find that you experience doubt*, validate that too. Because your limbic brain isn't used to having its feelings validated, it might respond with doubt or even cynicism. Validate absolutely everything including any nasty, shameful, angry, or critical feelings or thoughts you might sense inside you.

*Think about a how a child or a teenager would react the first time someone validates them if all they have ever experienced is the opposite. They are likely to respond at first with mistrust or even suspicion. This isn't familiar, it is not wired in yet. Your limbic brain reacts the same way. It'll take a lot of repetition before a child or teenager would get used to their feelings handled differently. Even a positive change requires adjustment. Practice will enable your neurones to become wired permanently, which is what 'getting used to something' really means.

- Repeat this practice every time you feel *anything*, especially feelings that are not comfortable. You might have to do this many times every day. Over time as your brain becomes wired to do this it will become second nature and it will be a lot easier. We all have conversations inside our heads, but when it comes to our emotions they are not always the right kind of conversations. This practice will gradually help replace your existing inner conversations with the right ones.

- If you are experiencing anxiety but have no idea what other emotions you might have, follow the same practice and validate your anxiety ('It's OK to feel anxious'). At first you won't know what feelings are behind your anxiety, but over time you will find out.

Important notes about this practice

- Some people find it useful to write down their experience and this includes the validation itself. If writing is for you, you might find that you can validate your own feelings more easily in writing.

- All exercise and practice suggestions are a starting point. If you find that the practice changes a bit over time, that's OK. Let it happen. You don't need to feel like you have to follow my directions in a rigid way. It's best if you adapt the practice to fit with your particular style and your own needs.

40

- The purpose of the exercise is *not to change how you feel*! The purpose is to wire your brain to learn to validate everything you feel. Your feelings need to finish their natural cycle. You need to learn to *listen* to what they tell you and, where appropriate and necessary, to act on the information they provide.

- It's important to remember that the purpose of any exercise you attempt is not just to get the result you are after. Even more important than whether or not you succeed in the short term, is to improve your self-awareness. There is no change without awareness! As you attempt this exercise don't worry so much about whether or not you succeeded. Pay attention to *what it's like for you to try to do this.* Is it easy? Is it difficult? Is it easier sometimes, and more difficult at other times? If so, what is the difference in the experience? In what way are the circumstances different, and in what way are *you* different when it's easier or more difficult? What else do you notice about yourself as you begin to practice this? If at some point you decide to see a therapist or if you are already seeing one, you can take the results of your observations to your therapy sessions and process them with your therapist.

- It's important to become protective of your feelings. Notice when others try to change, or 'fix' how your feel, or if they question or criticise your feelings. Even with the best of intentions people can get it wrong. They think they are helping but trying to change someone else's emotions not only doesn't work, it's also never helpful. It's more likely to leave people feeling alone and will ultimately contribute to their anxiety. It's OK and often necessary to let others know if something they do or say isn't helpful to you.

- All our feelings are OK, but not all of our behaviours are OK. Learn to notice the difference between feeling something and acting on that feeling.

Practicing emotional validation with children and young people

If you find it initially difficult to do this practice with yourself, it helps to start with children and young people. As you do it with them and as you see how it affects them it might become easier to begin to practice with yourself.

If you have children or young people in your life, or if you work with children of any age as a teacher, or in any other capacity, it helps to start practicing validation of emotions with them. If a child or a young person demonstrates an emotion, or communicates an emotion verbally, drill yourself to validate first. ('It's OK to feel like this.') Then see what happens…

You might find it difficult at first, because you might be in the habit of cracking a joke when someone says how they feel, you might feel annoyed when a child or young adult feels sad or a bit sorry for themselves, or you might automatically try to 'make them feel better' or 'fix' what they feel. It does take practice, but practice is what we need to become skilled, (which is another way of saying wired. Practice helps our brain cells stay together and fire together more reliably until they form a permanent neural network).

When you get better at feeling your authentic feelings whatever they are, sadness, disappointment, hurt, pain, sadness, boredom, anger, fear, pleasure, joy, fun, or anything else, your anxiety levels will begin to drop. But as your real feelings underneath the anxiety become clearer, you will have to begin to attend to what they are trying to tell you. It's not going to be easy. After all, there are probably good reasons why you haven't faced them before.

You might find that your feelings are telling you that there are difficult and important decisions you have to make. Maybe it's about a job that does not fulfil you, or a work environment that isn't good for you. Maybe you're not happy in a relationship, or maybe there are problems with one of your friendships, or maybe there is something from your past you need to attend to, or unfinished grief or a secret you have been keeping that has been bothering you at the back of your mind. Your feelings are always there for a reason and they always have something to tell you.

If you have suffered trauma at any time in your life, some of the feelings you will have to face could be especially difficult. One of the symptoms of Post-Traumatic Stress (PTS) is chronic anxiety. If this is your situation, it is a good idea to do this work with the help of a supportive and skilled therapist.

All skilled therapists should know how to work with feelings. Good therapists need to be prepared and able to join their clients wherever they are emotionally. To be able to do this, therapists have to be OK with their own feelings. If therapists avoid their own feelings they aren't likely to be helpful to their clients. Therapists who avoid their own feelings and issues can also be unsafe to work with. It's OK to ask therapists how they are taking care of their own emotions, and what they do to attend to their own personal development and growth.

The price of letting go of anxiety is that you'll have to be honest with yourself. You will not only learn to tolerate your feelings. You will learn to accept them. In the long term, you will welcome them as a valuable source of information that's there to help you live your life better, and as an important part of what makes you who you are.

About the author

Avigail Abarbanel has been a psychotherapist in private practice since 1999. She started practicing in Australia, and in 2010 moved to the north of Scotland, where she re-established her practice near Inverness. Avigail works with individuals, relationships, families and groups and as a trainer and workshop facilitator. She is also a clinical supervisor and a writer and is accredited with the BACP and with COSCA.

Registered Member **16797**
MBACP (Accred)

Visit http://fullyhuman.co.uk for more information about Avigail and her work.

Printed in Great Britain
by Amazon

82434941R00031